MW00744203

a gift for: _____

from: _____

Sister

Published by Sellers Publishing, Inc.
Copyright © 2010 Sellers Publishing, Inc.
Photography © 2010 Kendra Dew
All rights reserved.

Text by Ellen Pill
Edited by Robin Haywood

161 John Roberts Road, South Portland, Maine 04106
For ordering information:
(800) 625-3386 Toll free
(207) 772-6814 Fax
Visit our Web site: www.sellerspublishing.com
E-mail: rsp@rsvp.com

ISBN: 13: 978-1-4162-0601-9

10 9 8 7 6 5 4 3 2 1

Printed and bound in China.

Sister

WHAT WOULD I DO WITHOUT YOU?

PHOTOGRAPHY BY KENDRA DEW

SELLERS
PUBLISHING

*Sister, you always encouraged
me to dream big . . .*

*even though sometimes
it seemed as if we'd
never grow up.*

We shared everything —
ice cream and giggles . . .

. . . the latest dirt . . .

. . . and quiet moments
when we were feeling
a little blue.

We got into mischief together . . .

. . . and my favorite part was blaming it all on you!

*I could always trust you with
the name of my latest crush.*

Well . . . almost always.

*I admit there were times
I wished you'd disappear.*

But I was always relieved when you didn't.

*You helped me learn
how to be myself.*

Remember the lazy days
when it was just
you 'n me . . .

a little girly polish . . .

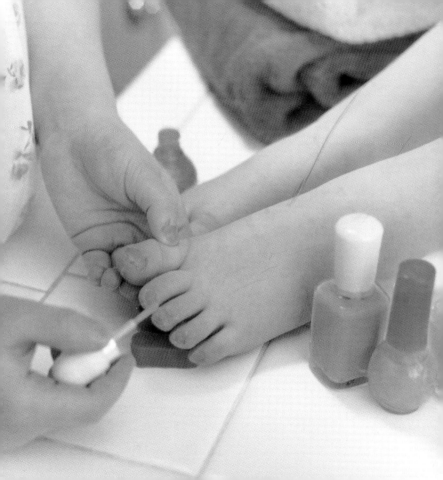

and a whole lot of silly?

You still know when
I need a little push
to get going.

Sometimes I'd think
you were an angel,

and sometimes I didn't.

Yet I knew you'd always
be there for me . . .

*. . . even when my world
turned upside down.*

Everything made us laugh,

but, you never laughed at me
when I shared my secrets . . .

even when I kept the
cookies all to myself.

I may have borrowed your clothes,
but I could never fill your shoes.

You even understood
when I had to go off
by myself . . .

and just be me alone.

*Yet I'm never quite complete
without you beside me.*

I love how we're two of a kind yet completely unique.

I don't know what
I'd do without you,

my forever friend.
My sister.

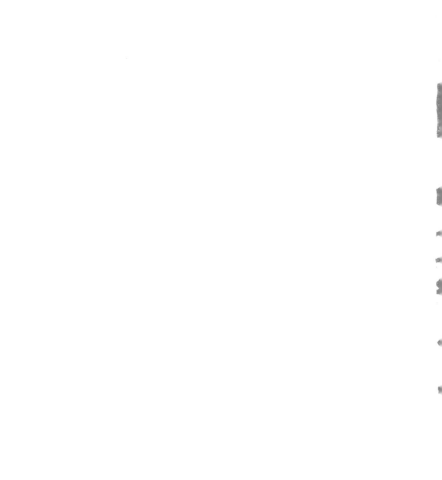